THE INDIAN FESTIVALS OF FLOWERS

AN INSIGHT INTO THE SIGNIFICANCE AND CELEBRATIONS OF INDIA'S FESTIVALS OF FLOWERS

DR. JAGADEESH PILLAI

Copyright © Dr. Jagadeesh Pillai
All Rights Reserved.

This book has been self-published with all reasonable efforts taken to make the material error-free by the author. No part of this book shall be used, reproduced in any manner whatsoever without written permission from the author, except in the case of brief quotations embodied in critical articles and reviews.

The Author of this book is solely responsible and liable for its content including but not limited to the views, representations, descriptions, statements, information, opinions and references ["Content"]. The Content of this book shall not constitute or be construed or deemed to reflect the opinion or expression of the Publisher or Editor. Neither the Publisher nor Editor endorse or approve the Content of this book or guarantee the reliability, accuracy or completeness of the Content published herein and do not make any representations or warranties of any kind, express or implied, including but not limited to the implied warranties of merchantability, fitness for a particular purpose. The Publisher and Editor shall not be liable whatsoever for any errors, omissions, whether such errors or omissions result from negligence, accident, or any other cause or claims for loss or damages of any kind, including without limitation, indirect or consequential loss or damage arising out of use, inability to use, or about the reliability, accuracy or sufficiency of the information contained in this book.

Made with ♥ on the Notion Press Platform
www.notionpress.com

|| "Dedicated to all who seek to understand and appreciate Indian culture and tradition." ||

Contents

Contents

PRAYER

"Om Bhadram Karnebbhih Shrunuyaama DevaahBhadram Pashyemaakshabhiryajatraah Sthirairangaistushtuvaamsastanoobhih Vyashema Devahitam YadaayuhSwasti Na Indro VridhashravaahSwasti Nah Pooshaa VishwavedaahSwasti Nastaarkshyo ArishtanemihSwasti No Brihaspatir DadhaatuOm Shantih, Shantih, Shantih"

The literal meaning of this mantra is: OM. O Gods! Let us hear auspicious words from our ears. O reverent Gods! Let us behold propitious visions from our eyes, let our organs and body be stable, healthy, and strong. Let us do that which is pleasing to the gods in the life span allotted to us. May Indra, inscribed in the scriptures, bring us fortune! May Pushan, the knower of the world, grant us prosperity! May Trakshya, who vanquishes enemies, bestow us with blessings! May Brihaspati bring us success!
OM Peace, Peace, Peace.

About The Author

Dr. Jagadeesh Pillai is a renowned Guinness World Record holder, writer, and researcher hailing from Varanasi, also known as the abode of Lord Shiva. With a Ph.D. in Vedic Science and a range of creative ideas and achievements, he is a true polymath. He is the author of more than 100 books including Research Publications. Although his roots can be traced back to Kerala, the people of Varanasi hold him in high regard and affectionately consider him one of their own.

Dr. Pillai has achieved four Guinness World Records in the following subjects:

"Script to Screen" - In this record, Dr. Pillai produced and directed an animation film within the shortest time possible, breaking the previous record set by Canadians. He has also received numerous national and international awards and recognitions for this achievement.

Longest Line of Postcards - For this record, Dr. Pillai created a line of 16,300 postcards on the occasion of the 163rd anniversary of Indian Postal Day. The event also included a questionnaire about the Indian flag.

Largest Poster Awareness Campaign - Dr. Pillai designed an awareness campaign on the subject of "Beti Bachao - Beti Padhao" (Save the Girl Child - Educate the Girl Child) to achieve this record.

Largest Envelope - In tribute to the Indian Prime Minister's

"Make in India" initiative, Dr. Pillai created a 4000 square meter envelope using waste paper to achieve this record.

Attempted - **70000 Candles on a 210 kg Cake** - To celebrate the 70th Indian Independence Day, Dr. Pillai attempted to light 70,000 candles on a 210 kg cake, which was recorded in World Records India.

Attempted - **Documentary on Dhamek Stupa of Sarnath in 17 Languages** - Dr. Pillai attempted to create a documentary on the Dhamek Stupa of Sarnath, dubbing it in 17 different languages. The result of this attempt is currently awaiting confirmation from the Guinness World Records.

Dr. Pillai is skilled in teaching the Bhagavad Gita, a Hindu scripture, and is popular among young people. He has helped many young people improve their lives through his motivational teachings.

In addition to teaching, he has composed and sung numerous Sanskrit Bhajans and patriotic songs.

He has also written and directed several short films and documentaries for awareness campaigns, and has volunteered with the police in both UP and Kerala to spread awareness about various issues through videos and photography.

Incredibly, he has produced and directed over 100 documentaries about the city of Varanasi, all on his own.

He has also helped and guided more than 25 boys and girls to achieve world records through creative and innovative methods. He is a multifaceted person who uses his intellect and the blessings given to him by God to excel in various areas. He is both a teacher and a student, always learning and teaching, and is able to master any subject he comes across.

He is a selfless social activist and motivational speaker who has overcome struggles and failures to become a successful and enthusiastic individual with a rich life experience.

In addition to his work with the Bhagavad Gita, he is also an efficient Tarot card reader, Astro-Vastu consultant, and a talented singer and composer. He has sung the entire Ram Charita Manas and Bhagavad Gita in his own compositions, and has sung the phrase "Lokah Samastha Sukhino Bhavantu" in 50 different languages. He is currently working on a detailed and scientific study of Vedas, Upanishads, Puranas, and the Bhagavad Gita. He has also composed and sung the Hanuman Chalisa and Gayatri Mantra in 108 and 1008 different compositions, respectively.

Awards - Four Times Guinness World Records, Winner of Mahatma Gandhi Vishwa Shanti Puraskar, Mahatma Gandhi Global Peace Ambassador, Kashi Ratna Award, Dr. APJ Abdul Kalam Motivational Person of the Year 2017, Mother Teresa Award, Indira Gandhi Priyadarshini Award, Bharat Vikas Ratna Award, Udyog Ratna Award, Vigyan Prasar Award, Poorvanchal Ratn Samman.

PREFACE

India is renowned for its rich and vibrant culture, and its festivals of flowers are no exception. These festivals of flowers are a celebration of the beauty, color, and life that flowers bring to the world. This book, The Indian Festivals of Flowers: An Insight into the Significance and Celebrations of India's Festivals of Flowers, seeks to explore the significance and celebrations of India's festivals of flowers.

This book is intended to serve as an introduction to the rich history and culture of the Indian festivals of flowers for readers who are new to the subject. It explores the significance of flowers in Indian culture, popular festivals of flowers in India, and Holi: the Festival of Colors. It also examines the Rose Festival in Chandigarh, the International Flower Festival in Gangtok, the Spring Valley Flower Festival in Kashmir, the Tulip Festival in Srinagar, the Kaas Plateau Flower Festival, and the Ooty Flower Show.

The book draws on research from a variety of sources, including interviews with key figures in the Indian flower festivals industry, archival materials, and cultural analysis. I have also conducted extensive field research in India, including attending flower festivals, interviewing flower vendors, and visiting locations associated with the production of flowers. Through this research, I hope to provide readers with a comprehensive understanding of the Indian flower festivals industry and its various components.

I am deeply passionate about the beauty of Indian flower festivals and hope that this book will help to spread the appreciation of this wonderful form of celebration. I believe that the Indian festivals of flowers have a great deal to offer to the world and I am excited to share their cultural and historical significance with my readers.

I

Introduction to the Indian Festivals of Flowers

India is a land of vibrant colors and festivals, and one such unique festival that is celebrated in India is the Festival of Flowers. This is an ancient festival that is celebrated in many parts of India and is often associated with the beauty of nature. The festival is celebrated with much enthusiasm, and the beauty of colorful flowers is an integral part of the celebration. The festival is an important part of the culture of India and has been celebrated for centuries.

The Festival of Flowers is celebrated in various parts of India, and each region has its own unique way of celebrating the festival. In some parts of the country, the festival is celebrated for two days and in other parts for a week. During the festival, people decorate their homes and streets with flowers and use them as offerings to the gods.

The use of flowers in religious ceremonies is also common in many parts of India.

The Festival of Flowers is usually celebrated in the month of November or December and is accompanied by various rituals and customs. The most popular ritual during the festival is the offering of flowers to the gods and goddesses. People make offerings of flowers at the local temples and seek blessings from the divine. The offering of flowers is believed to bring good luck and fortune.

Apart from the offering of flowers, there are other activities associated with the festival. People sing and dance in the streets and enjoy the beauty of the colorful flowers. Special sweets are also prepared and distributed among the people as a way of celebrating the festival.

The Festival of Flowers is a time of celebration, joy and happiness. It is a time to appreciate the beauty of nature and to celebrate the spirit of unity and brotherhood. The festival is a unique way of celebrating the culture and customs of India, and it is an important part of the Indian culture.

"Indian festivals are a celebration of life and its many colors."

ꕤ

II

The Significance of Flowers in Indian Culture

The significance of flowers in Indian culture has been known since ancient times. From the spiritual significance of offering flowers in religious ceremonies to the use of flowers in marriages and other celebrations, flowers have been an integral part of Indian culture.

In Hindu mythology, flowers have been associated with the gods and goddesses. For example, Goddess Lakshmi is often depicted seated on a pink lotus flower, and Goddess Saraswati is often depicted seated on a white lotus flower. In Indian culture, the lotus flower represents divinity, fertility, wealth, knowledge, and enlightenment.

In addition to religious ceremonies, flowers are also used in many other aspects of Indian culture. In particular, flowers are often used in weddings. In the pre-wedding ceremonies, turmeric powder mixed with essential oils like jasmine and rose are used to beautify the bride and groom. During the wedding ceremony, the bride and groom exchange garlands made of flowers. In Southern India, the Onam festival is celebrated with the preparation of a flower carpet or rangoli in the front courtyard.

Flowers are also used in other events such as anniversaries and birthdays. The most popular flower for these occasions is the red rose, which symbolises love and romance. On Valentine's Day, people often give flowers to their loved ones.

In India, flowers have long been used to express emotions and feelings. For example, a jasmine flower is often given to express love and admiration. The tulsi leaf is a symbol of purity and is often offered to the gods in Hindu rituals. The manjaris are used in yogic practices, and have medicinal value.

Flowers play an important role in Indian culture. They have been used in religious ceremonies, weddings, and other important events, and they are often used to express emotions and feelings. Flowers are a symbol of unity, diversity, liveliness, and generosity, and they provide the country with a rich cultural fragrance and values.

"The diversity of Indian festivals reflects the diversity of its people and culture."

ꕤ

III

Popular Festivals of Flowers in India

Flowers are an integral part of our culture and festivals in India. There are numerous festivals in India which are celebrated with much fanfare, and the use of flowers in such occasions adds to the beauty of the celebrations. From the north to the south and from the east to the west, people in India celebrate festivals with flowers, and some festivals are even dedicated to flowers. In this essay, we will discuss some of the popular flower festivals of India.

First, we will talk about the famous festival of Holi. Holi is celebrated in the month of Phalguna (March) and is known as the 'Festival of Colors'. People play with colors, splash each other with colored water and also exchange sweets and flowers. The whole atmosphere is filled with the spirit of joy and happiness. The use of flowers during this festival adds to the beauty and vibrancy of the celebration.

Another popular flower festival is Phoolon Wali Holi, celebrated in the state of Rajasthan. This festival is celebrated on the full moon night of Phalguna. During this festival, people exchange flowers and shower each other with petals. The fragrant flowers used in this festival are known as 'Gulal'.

The festival of Basant Panchami is also celebrated with great enthusiasm in India. This festival is celebrated in the month of Magha (February) and marks the beginning of spring season. On this day, people wear yellow clothes and exchange flowers. The use of yellow flowers is considered auspicious and is a way of welcoming the new season.

Gulal Utsav is another flower festival which is celebrated in the state of Gujarat. This festival is celebrated in the month of Chaitra (April) and is a two-day celebration. During this festival, people wear colorful clothes and exchange flowers. People also take out a procession in the streets and sprinkle colored water on each other.

The festival of Pushkar is celebrated in the month of Kartik (November) and is a major event in Rajasthan. During this festival, devotees visit the Pushkar Lake and offer flowers to their gods and goddesses. The use of flowers in this festival is considered highly auspicious and is a way of offering prayers to the deities.

Last but not least, the festival of Rakhi is celebrated in the month of Shravan (August). This festival.

"Indian festivals bring people together, breaking down barriers and fostering unity."

ꟼ

IV

Holi: The Festival of Colors

Holi is one of the most celebrated festivals in India. It is celebrated during the spring season and is considered to be a festival of joy and happiness. Holi is traditionally celebrated by applying colors to each other and by playing with water. It is also known as the 'Festival of Colors'.

The origin of Holi can be traced back to the legend of Holika and Prahlad. According to Hindu mythology, Prahlad was the son of Hiranyakashipu, who was a tyrant king. Hiranyakashipu was so jealous of his son's devotion to Lord Vishnu that he decided to kill him. But, due to the divine intervention of Lord Vishnu, Prahlad was saved from his father's wrath. The burning of Holika in the fire is celebrated as Holi.

Holi is celebrated in many parts of India. In the North, Holi is celebrated with the burning of Holika and other rituals.

People smear each other with color and water and sing and dance in the streets. In the South, Holi is celebrated with the worship of Lord Krishna and the playing of music and dance. In the East, Holi is celebrated with a variety of customs, such as the flying of kites and the singing of devotional songs.

The use of flowers is also an important aspect of Holi celebrations. In many parts of India, colorful flowers are used to decorate the houses and the streets. People exchange flowers and garlands as a symbol of love and friendship. Different types of flowers are used in Holi, such as marigold, hibiscus, and chrysanthemums.

Holi is also celebrated with the exchange of gifts and sweets. People exchange sweets, such as burfi and peda, as a symbol of love and affection. The exchange of gifts is also an important part of Holi celebrations. People exchange gifts, such as clothes and jewelry, to show their appreciation for each other.

Holi is a wonderful festival that brings people together and spreads joy and happiness. It is a time when people forget their differences and come together to celebrate the spirit of love and friendship. The use of flowers in Holi celebrations adds to the beauty and vibrancy of the festival.

"In India, festivals are not just a time for celebration, but also a time for reflection and renewal."

℘

V

The Rose Festival in Chandigarh

The Rose Festival in Chandigarh is one of the most popular and eagerly awaited festivals in India. This festival is celebrated at the Zakir Hussain Rose Garden in Sector 16 of Chandigarh. The festival was established in the year 1947 and is now celebrated every year.

The Rose Festival is an event dedicated to the beauty and magnificence of roses. There are several thousand species of rose bushes growing in the Zakir Hussain Rose Garden. The festival showcases a wide variety of hybrid roses such as teas rose, miniature rose, climber rose, green rose, and many more. Roses are named after famous personalities like Zakir Hussain, Queen Elizabeth, John F. Kennedy, Delhi, and so on.

The festival not only puts on display the exquisite roses and other flowers but also many other attractions and entertainment for the visitors. The other activities are; Folk dances, Mr. and Miss Rose competition, Traditional dance competitions, Short plays, Flower cutting and arrangement contests. The festival also features helicopter rides, a great way to get a bird's eye view of the beautiful rose garden.

The Rose Festival is also a great opportunity for the people to learn about the importance of nature and its conservation. There are various awareness programs conducted during the festival which include talks and discussions about the environment and its conservation. The 2019 floral festival celebration had a transgender awareness program.

The Rose Festival of Chandigarh is a great way to bring people together and appreciate the beauty of nature. The festival is celebrated with much enthusiasm and joy, and the use of flowers adds to the beauty and vibrancy of the celebration. Thousands of people visit the festival every year, and the number of visitors and participants increases every year. The Rose Festival of Chandigarh is a great way to pay tribute to the beauty of nature and the magnificence of roses.

"Indian festivals are a reminder of the rich history and traditions of the country."

ꕥ

VI

The International Flower Festival in Gangtok

The International Flower Festival in Gangtok is one of the most popular and sought after festivals in India. The festival is celebrated in the state of Sikkim in the month of May and is a primary source of attraction among the tourists as well as the local inhabitants. The festival is organised by the Government of Sikkim and showcases a wide variety of flowers including orchids, gladioli, roses, cacti, alpine plants, creepers, climbers, ferns, herbs, and many more.

The International Flower Festival is held in the Flower Exhibition Centre in Gangtok, where hundreds of species of flowers are put on display. The flower show is accompanied by a food festival, where one may try several local delicacies. The event also includes a variety of activities such as lectures and seminars held by renowned botanical scientists and river rafting experience.

The festival is a great way to learn about the importance of conservation of nature and its beauty. Different awareness programs are conducted during the festival which include talks and discussions about the environment and its conservation. The festival also helps in increasing tourism in the state as it serves as a platform to promote the diverse culture of Sikkim.

The International Flower Festival in Gangtok is a great way to bring people together and appreciate the beauty of nature. The festival is celebrated with much enthusiasm and joy, and the use of flowers adds to the beauty and vibrancy of the celebration. Thousands of people visit the festival every year, and the number of visitors and participants increases every year. The International Flower Festival in Gangtok is a great way to pay tribute to the beauty of nature and the magnificence of flowers.

"The vibrant colors and joyous celebrations of Indian festivals are a feast for the senses."

ꕥ

VII

The Spring Valley Flower Festival in Kashmir

The Spring Valley Flower Festival in Kashmir is one of the most popular festivals in India. The festival is held in the spring season, from the middle of April to the beginning of May. The festival is a celebration of nature's beauty and is an occasion to appreciate the vibrant and colorful flowers of Kashmir.

The festival is held in the Valley of Flowers in Kashmir, which is known for its lush green meadows and beautiful flowers. During the festival, the valley is filled with a variety of flowers such as roses, daisies, tulips, lilies, and many more. The festival also features a variety of cultural activities such as music, dance, and theatre performances.

The festival is also a great opportunity for the people to

learn about the importance of nature and its conservation. There are various awareness programs conducted during the festival which include talks and discussions about the environment and its conservation. The festival also features a variety of competitions like flower arranging, flower photography, and flower show.

The Spring Valley Flower Festival in Kashmir is a great way to bring people together and appreciate the beauty of nature. The festival is celebrated with much enthusiasm and joy, and the use of flowers adds to the beauty and vibrancy of the celebration. Thousands of people visit the festival every year, and the number of visitors and participants increases every year. The Spring Valley Flower Festival in Kashmir is a great way to pay tribute to the beauty of nature and the magnificence of flowers.

"Indian festivals are a celebration of the cycle of life and death, and the connection between the two."

ഗ

VIII

The Tulip Festival in Srinagar

The Tulip Festival in Srinagar is one of the most celebrated festivals in India. The festival is held every year in April, and it celebrates the blooming season of tulips in the Kashmir Valley. The festival is organized by the Government of Jammu and Kashmir, and it showcases a wide variety of tulips such as Fringed Tulip, Parrot Tulip, Fosteriana Tulip, and many more.

The Tulip Festival is held at the Indira Gandhi Memorial Tulip Garden in Srinagar, which is spread over 30 hectares with 1.5 million tulip bulbs of 62 varieties and also features a large variety of other flowers such as daffodils, hyacinths, and narcissus. The festival also includes a variety of cultural activities such as folk dances, short plays, flower cutting and arrangement competitions, and helicopter rides.

The Tulip Festival is not only a great way to appreciate the beauty of nature but also a great opportunity for the people to learn about the importance of nature and its conservation. There are various awareness programs conducted during the festival which include talks and discussions about the environment and its conservation.

The Tulip Festival in Srinagar is a great way to bring people together and appreciate the beauty of nature. The festival is celebrated with much enthusiasm and joy, and the use of flowers adds to the beauty and vibrancy of the celebration. Thousands of people visit the festival every year, and the number of visitors and participants increases every year. The Tulip Festival in Srinagar is a great way to pay tribute to the beauty of nature and the magnificence of tulips.

"The diversity of Indian festivals is a reflection of the country's diverse religions and communities."

ᴕ

IX

The Kaas Plateau Flower Festival

The Kaas Plateau Flower Festival is an annual event held in the month of August-September in the Kaas Plateau of Maharashtra, India. The festival is celebrated with great enthusiasm and joy, and it is a great opportunity for the people to appreciate the beauty of nature and the magnificence of flowers.

The Kaas Plateau is home to over 850 species of wild flowers and plants and it has been declared a UNESCO World Heritage Site. During the festival, the plateau comes alive with a variety of flowers such as orchids, daisies, lilies, roses, and many more. The festival also features a variety of cultural activities such as music, dance, and theatre performances.

The festival is also a great platform to learn about the importance of nature and its conservation. There are various awareness programs conducted during the festival which include talks and discussions about the environment and its conservation. The festival also features a variety of competitions like flower arranging, flower photography, and flower show.

The Kaas Plateau Flower Festival is a great way to bring people together and appreciate the beauty of nature. The festival is celebrated with much enthusiasm and joy, and the use of flowers adds to the beauty and vibrancy of the celebration. Thousands of people visit the festival every year, and the number of visitors and participants increases every year. The Kaas Plateau Flower Festival is a great way to pay tribute to the beauty of nature and the magnificence of flowers.

"Indian festivals are a way for people to come together and celebrate their shared culture and heritage."

ꕤ

X

The Ooty Flower Show

The Ooty Flower Show is one of the most popular festivals in India. The festival is held in the month of May in the Queen of Hills - Ooty. The Ooty Flower Show is conducted in the Government Botanical Garden, and it is a great way to appreciate the beauty of nature and the magnificence of flowers.

The Ooty Flower Show showcases a variety of flowers such as roses, carnations, lilies, and many more. The festival also features a variety of cultural activities such as music, dance, and theatre performances. The event also encourages young artists to showcase their work and provides them with a platform to showcase their talent.

The Ooty Flower Show is also a great platform to learn about the importance of nature and its conservation. There are various awareness programs conducted during the festival which include talks and discussions about the environment and its conservation. The festival also features a variety of competitions like flower arranging, flower photography, and flower show.

The Ooty Flower Show is a great way to bring people together and appreciate the beauty of nature. The festival is celebrated with much enthusiasm and joy, and the use of flowers adds to the beauty and vibrancy of the celebration. Thousands of people visit the festival every year, and the number of visitors and participants increases every year. The Ooty Flower Show is a great way to pay tribute to the beauty of nature and the magnificence of flowers.

"The bright lights and lively music of Indian festivals create a joyous and festive atmosphere."

ꙮ

XI

Experiencing Indian Flower Festivals

India is known for its diverse cultural heritage, and the nation is celebrated for its vibrant festivals. One such festival is the flower festival, which is celebrated in various parts of the country. Flower festivals are a great way to experience the beauty of nature and appreciate the magnificence of flowers.

India is home to numerous flower festivals, and they are celebrated with much enthusiasm and joy. The festivals feature a variety of flowers such as roses, carnations, lilies, and many more. The festivals also feature a variety of cultural activities such as music, dance, and theatre performances. The festivals also provide a platform to the young artists to showcase their work and provide them with a platform to showcase their talent.

These festivals also provide a great platform to learn about the importance of nature and its conservation. There are various awareness programs conducted during the festivals which include talks and discussions about the environment and its conservation. The festivals also feature a variety of competitions like flower arranging, flower photography, and flower show.

Attending the Indian flower festivals is a great way to bring people together and appreciate the beauty of nature. The festivals are celebrated with much enthusiasm and joy, and the use of flowers adds to the beauty and vibrancy of the celebration. Thousands of people visit the festivals every year, and the number of visitors and participants increases every year. Experiencing Indian flower festivals is a great way to pay tribute to the beauty of nature and the magnificence of flowers.

Other Books Of The Author

1. The Moments When I Met God
2. Kashiyile Theertha Pathangal
3. GURU GYAN VANI
4. Abhiprerak Gita
5. ASSI SE JAIN GHAT TAK
6. Hopelessness of Arjuna
7. The Soul and It's True Nature
8. Sense of Action (Karma)
9. Action through Wisdom
10. Action through Wisdom
11. THEORY AND PRACTICAL OF EVERY ACTION
12. LOGICAL UNDERSTANDING OF THE SUPREME
13. THE IMPERISHABLE SUPREME
14. Yatra Nishadraj se Hanuman Ghat Tak
15. Yatra Karnatak Ghat se Raja Ghat Tak
16. Yatra Pandey Ghat se Prayagraj Ghat Tak
17. Yatra Ranjendra Prasad Ghat se Dattatreya Ghat Tak
18. YaatraSindhiya Ghat se Gwaliar Ghat Tak
19. Yatra Mangala Gauri Ghat se Hanuman Gadhi Ghat Tak
20. Yatra Gaay Ghat Se Nishad Ghat Tak
21. MAA GANGA, GHATEN EVM UTSAV
22. Ganga Arti Dev Deepavali evam Any Utsav
23. Potentials of Digitalized India
24. VEDIC CONSCIOUSNESS
25. A Brief Introduction to Vedic Science
26. Kashi ke Barah Jyotirling
27. IMPACT OF MOTIVATION
28. Let's have a Milky Way Journey
29. Color Therapy in a Nutshell

30. Rigveda in a Nutshell
31. Yajurveda in a Nutshell
32. Samveda in a Nutshell
33. Atharva Veda in a Nutshell
34. Ayushman Bhava - Ayurveda
35. Srimad Bhagavad Gita and Upanishad Connection
36. Srimad Bhagavad Gita - an attempt to summarize each chapter.
37. Facts and Impact of Nakshatra
38. Astro Gems - NAVARATNA
39. Ekadashi - A Concise Overview
40. A Concise View of Hanuman Chalisa
41. Inspirational Gita
42. Nakshatraranyam
43. Summary of 18 Mahapuranas
44. Synopsis of 18 Upa Puranas
45. Rigvediya Upanishads
46. Shukla Yajurvediya Upanishads
47. Krishna Yajurvediya Upanishads
48. Samavediya Upanishads
49. Atharvavediya Upanishads
50. The Seven Great Sages
51. From Rocket Scientist to President Dr. APJ Abdul Kalam
52. The Visionary's Voice - Quotes of Dr. APJ Abdul Kalam
53. The Wisdom of Swami Vivekananda: Insights and Inspiration from a Legendary Spiritual Teacher
54. Ayurvedic Remedies from the Garden
55. Sages and Seers
56. Rising Strong – Motivational Stories of Women
57. Beyond Flames -Mystery stories of Funeral Ghat Manikarnika
58. The Origins of Tulsi: A Look at the Mythological Roots of the Plant"

59. The Holistic Cow: A Look at the Physical, Spiritual, and Cultural Importance of Cows in India
60. Arts of Healing
61. Exploring the Divine
62. Understanding Five Elements
63. The Etymology of Ram
64. Symbols of India
65. Voice of Change (About Speeches of Great Men)
66. She Speaks (About Speeches of Great Women)
67. Patriotism on Celluloid – Brief About Patriotic Films
68. The Music of Motivation: A Brief Guide to Inspirational Film Songs
69. **Unlocking the Secrets of the Dashopanishads**
70. A Cultural Mosaic
71. Ancient Traditions, Modern Minds
72. Ecos of Ancient Wisdom
73. Beneath the Surface
74. From Temples to Ashrams
75. Sages of the Subcontinent
76. The Art of Healling (Ayurveda, Yoga & Naturopathy)
77. Indian Kitchen
78. The Festivals of India
79. The Indian Epics Retold
80. The Power of Mantras
81. The Indian River Ganges
82. The Indian Architecture
83. Rites of Passage
84. The Indian Silk Road
85. The Indian Literature
86. The Indian Villages
87. The Indian Folks & Crafts
88. The Way of Buddha
89. The Ramayan of Tulsidas

90. Astrological Remedies
91. The Secret Power of Motivation
92. Secret of Developing your Inner Strength
93. The Secret Path to Motivation
94. The Art and Secret of Positive Thinking
95. The Secrets of Practicing Ethical Living
96. Indian Art and Painting
97. The Indian Herbalism
98. Bharatanatyam to Kathak
99. Exploring India's Astrological Remedies

DR. JAGADEESH PILLAI

PhD in Vedic Science

Four Times Guinness World Record Holder

Winner of Mahatma Gandhi Vishwa Shanti Puraskar and
Global Peace Ambassador

Gemology, Astro & Vastu Consultant - Spiritual Counselor

Consultant for designing World Record Ideas

Efficient Tarot Card Reader

9839093003

myrichindia@gmail.com

drjagadeeshpillai@facebook

drjagadeeshpillai@instagram

jagadeeshpillai@youtube

www. JAGADEESHPILLAI.com

ꕤ

|| LOKAHA SAMASTHAHA SUKHINO BHAVANTU ||

9 798889 515869

Printed by Libri Plureos GmbH in Hamburg, Germany